T0128429

Having a Successful Life Being Led by the Holy Spirit

What's the Use of Having the Holy Ghost If You're Not Going to Obey Him

Bishop William A. Mitchell Jr.

WESTBOW
P R E S S®
A DIVISION OF THOMAS NELSON
& ZONDERVAN

All Scripture quotations are taken from the King James Version

WestBow Press books may be ordered through booksellers or by contacting:

WestBow Press
A Division of Thomas Nelson & Zondervan
1663 Liberty Drive
Bloomington, IN 47403
www.westbowpress.com
1 (866) 928-1240

ISBN: 978-1-9736-5668-5 (sc)
ISBN: 978-1-9736-5667-8 (e)

Print information available on the last page.

WestBow Press rev. date: 05/02/2019

I dedicate this book to my darling wife Myrtle,
my beloved parents,
Pastor Hilda G. Mitchell,
And Deacon William A. Mitchell Sr.
and Bishop J. E. Reddick,
of the
United American Free Will Baptist Denomination, Incorporated

Introduction

The Holy Spirit can be a very powerful tool in your life. High school is where I initially felt God dealing with me. At the age of 16, I was fascinated when I felt God leading me to preach his word. When I heard God's voice within me, I felt he was saying, "You have got to preach my word." At the age of 53, I still hear his voice with that same intensity. After the initial call, my desire was to learn his commandments through his word. I wanted to know when, where, and how to preach his word.

As a Christian I have always tried to obey the Holy Spirit. Sometimes you miss what he is saying but don't worry, just keep on listening. Try the Spirit and see if it is of God. **"Beloved, believe not every spirit, but try the spirits whether they are of God; because many false prophets are gone out into the world. (KJV 1 John 4:1)"** The Holy Spirit will always take you slow, but don't grieve him. Often times you hear people say, **"Something told me to do this"**. Don't you know who it is that you're hearing within? As you mature in Christ you should be saying: "the Holy Spirit is leading me to do this or that".

The only way to know what God is leading you to do in the Spirit is to pray. Throughout my ministry I talk a lot about prayer. Prayer helps you to stay on track with the will of God. There are many false spirits in the world, and because of this, I'm afraid that the "Church" is missing a lot. At the same time some churches are hitting the mark. In the last days we will see **The Power of God** moving in a lot of ways, and simultaneously a move in the demonic realm will be taking place. **What's the use of having the Holy Ghost if you're not going to obey him?**

I believe the more we pray, and stay in God's word, we would know what he is saying to the church. This is what I'm trying to teach from writing this book: **Having A Successful Life Being Led By The Holy Spirit.** God has given us everything we need to conquer the enemy. This book will teach you a diversity of ways in which the Holy Spirit will deal with you and others.

Chapter One

Preparation

God has an amazingly powerful way, in which he deals with you through the Holy Spirit. As he begins to direct your path, to put you where he ultimately wants you to be, just obey. Where ever he leads you, by the way of the Holy Ghost, it is the place he wants you to be, to be a blessing to many people.

Looking back to the time when I was employed as a barber at Central Heights Barber Shop, I couldn't understand why I felt God leading me to leave my job, making $10.75 an hour (which was a lot of money at that time), to come back home. This was about 33 years ago. God had a two-fold anointing for me. I was to work in the barber shop, and in the ministry that God had called me to work. Don't ever despise what God is doing in your life. Each stage he takes you through, he is preparing you for the work he wants you to do. As I worked in the barber shop, God was preparing me for my destiny. What I didn't understand at that time, he began to reveal to me later, by the power of the Holy Ghost. I am thankful to God for that period now. What's the use of having the Holy Ghost if you're not going to obey him? What God wants to do in our lives is to be a guide to us through the Holy Ghost, and at the same time teach us discipline. Once we learn discipline, then God can use us for his will and his glory. For example, when I started my business at the barber shop, I didn't have a lot of customers, because I was a new barber. I had time to sit, read, and pray a lot. Even though business was slow, I never felt God leading me to go anywhere else to work. In the Barbering profession, you must stay there and work to build up a clientele. I stayed in the shop and waited for customers to come, whenever they decided to come, or when God would direct and lead them to come. Even in that, the word of God was teaching me discipline. I felt God leading me to sit and read my bible and pray when I didn't have customers. When customers did come in, I proceeded with my work. I did this daily. I read the bible, prayed and talked to God throughout the day each day when I did not have customers.

God continually dealt with me through dreams and visions. He was showing me how I would Pastor a church one day and the things he wanted me to do when that happened.

I couldn't see this because each day, I was sitting in a chair waiting for clientele to come in order for me to build my business, as a barber. At the same time, I felt God dealing with me about my Ministry and what I had to do for him.

As I worked in the barber shop, I could feel the Holy Spirit beginning to lead and guide me within. He was dealing with me about the things I had to do in the Ministry.

When the Holy Ghost begins to reveal powerful things to you, always believe what he is saying and doing in your life. God is a God that cannot lie. The truth lies within your loins. As I sat there, in the barber shop, God began to take me through times of preparation. I would just read, pray and talk to the almighty God.

A wide variety of people began to come to the barber shop. The barber shop became a place for me to learn about people.

I began to learn the different personalities; the different walks of life; what interested people, and what didn't. The customers would share whatever was on their minds. There is something about being in the barber shop that causes a person to share everything that they're going through in life. I began to listen and learn. What I didn't know at that time, but learned through his word and prayer, the Lord was teaching me how to counsel people, even while I was cutting their hair. He was also teaching me how to minister to people in a powerful way. He was teaching me how to be a good listener which makes a great counselor. I sat in the barber shop each day learning, reading God's word and listening. **What's the use of having the Holy Ghost if you're not going to obey him?**

Preparation and Discipline from reading God's word. God will take you and elevate you into a powerful realm of his, and then he will make sure he has all your heart. Not just your hands or your mind, all of you. **"Jesus said unto him, Thou shalt love the Lord thy God with all thy heart, and with all thy soul and with all thy mind." (KJV Matt. 22:37)** As I began to pray and talk to God, discipline began to develop in my life. On Wednesday nights we would have bible study at Greater St. John F.W.B. Church, the church I pastor. The bible studies became very powerful through the Holy Ghost, and they are still very powerful today. At this point in my life, my clientele at the shop had grown. Amazingly enough on Wednesday mornings before Bible Study, when I arrived at the barber shop, there were customers standing around the room waiting to get their hair cut.

My co-workers would ask me; "Rev are you going to Bible Study tonight are you going to stay here and cut hair?" I would see all these customers, who I felt was led by God to come to the shop, standing around the wall. I would say, "Nothing comes before me serving God."

I had the privilege of being able to obey God in this manner because I was self-employed. I would not recommend doing this if you work for an employer. We must obey the laws of the land according to the word.

After working two years in the shop I was promoted to manager-Master Barber. As the manager of the shop, I could set my own hours.

When I made the statement that God comes first, everyone would look at me in a strange way. The average person today would have thought about all the money that could be made today. Still I left the barber shop every Wednesday evening at 6 p.m. When you love God and God loves you, and there is an intimate relationship between the two of you, there is a powerful anointing upon your life. God's love will cause you to do his will. Do not let anything stop you or separate you from being in the ultimate presence of God. **What's the use of having the Holy Ghost if you're not going to obey him?**

When you feel the Holy Ghost is leading you, remember, he is always leading you into your next miracle. We all need the miracles of God to survive in this world. I would leave the shop and go to Wednesday night Bible Study and have no thought about the money I could have made in the shop that night. Are you ready for this powerful revelation? When you seek God nothing else matters. **"But seek ye first the kingdom of God And his righteousness; and all these things shall be added unto you"** **(KJV Matt. 6:33).** Each time I left the barber shop on Wednesdays to go to bible study, we would have a highly anointed time in the service. The next morning after bible study I would return to work and my co-workers would begin to talk about how they had to work hard and were unable to go home until 9 p.m., 10 p.m., and sometimes 11 p.m. You think I lost a lot of money? No, I did not. As we obey the Holy Spirit, the Lord gives us the spiritual as well as the natural blessings. Do you know the power of God through the manifestation of the Holy Spirit? If you do, then you know it is very awesome. You know that God will supply your needs, as you make a stand for him. Why can't we trust the Holy Spirit? Why can't we trust God? Why do we have to go through so many trials and many errors before we start obeying what God is leading us to do?

When I came back in the shop on Thursday morning, I had customers sitting around the wall waiting for "me". The other barbers were just sitting in their chairs. Look how good God is. He blessed them on Wednesday and now they're resting on Thursday from 7 a.m. to 12 p.m. or 1 p.m. They had no customers. This is what I felt God leading and guiding me to understand. If you're going to sacrifice things in order to worship, love, and praise me in your spiritual devotion by going to Bible Study and teaching his word, I will honor you by giving back to you everything the enemy wants you to think you've lost, and more.

Remember the story of Job, when the enemy took all he had, his children, livestock, his whole family and even his wife turned against him. Job held on to his integrity and his love for God. Job was given more, double, triple in comparison to what he had lost. This is what I was learning as I prayed, read his word and stayed in his will. So, I knew when I preached his word and lived for him, God was going to take care of me in a very powerful way.

On Thursdays I worked hard with my customers and the other barbers were amazed that their business was slow. That's the preparation that God was carrying me through.

The Holy Ghost will try his best to bring discipline in our lives, if we let him. However; sometimes we don't like to be disciplined, and I can understand that. We are like the children of Israel. They didn't like to be disciplined. But God kept right on until he found leaders that he could discipline for his will and his glory, in order that his people would be blessed. He also tried to find people that he could discipline to be good sheep that would follow the Shepherd that he had placed before them.

Prior to church services, I would go in my study in my home to pray and talk to God. As a result, during these services, the power of God would move mightily. You would not believe how the people were blessed. These results led me to pray to God more. As I prayed to him, I began to learn more under his anointing.

I would listen and talk to other Pastors. Their conversations would be about the things they have done; places that they traveled; and the people they have seen. I often spoke these words to God, "If I was a full time Pastor, I would seek your face day and night for your people." You must be careful with the vows you make to God, because the Holy Spirit and the power of God are listening to you. God will see just how much you really love him. After I told God that, I began to seek his face more. As I preached, many souls got saved.

The Evangelical anointing rested on me to the extent, that if God would lead me to preach a repentance message it would tear into the heart of every sinner in the congregation. They would all make their way to the altar and ask; "What must I do to be saved?" God's word teaches us if we believe in him, we would do the same works and even greater. I told God I believe in your son Jesus, and I can do the same works he did and even greater works, right here on earth. I prayed and asked God for an anointing to preach the word that many would get saved.

For seven years I preached to inmates in the prison system as part of my preparation. This was part of the preparation that God had ordained for my life. During the years that I ministered to the inmates, I became familiar with the personalities of the inmates and how the enemy was able to use them. It was this type of preparation that sharpened my skills of discernment. Discernment is needed, when a majority of everyone in prison declares: "I'm innocent." You need the power of the Holy Ghost to deal with the inmates. **What's the use of having the Holy Ghost if you're not going to obey him?**

It was during this period of time I felt God showing me how to minister and preach his word for more than 15 or 20 minutes. The prison system allowed us one hour to minister to the inmates. I had to minister the word to them the entire hour. On one occasion I went to the prison to preach, and I did not study. That was one of the toughest messages I ever had to preach. God's word tells us: to every man we should be able to give him an answer, and how can you give an answer if you have not prayed or studied your word accurately enough, that the Holy Ghost may move through you.

When we have a lot of "stuff" in our spirit, it dams up our spirit and the presence of the Holy Ghost will not flow. The Holy Spirit will not dwell in an unclean temple. The more I preached, and souls got saved; I realized that I was preaching by the power of the Holy Ghost. When he came upon me, many souls got saved.

I was not satisfied with this place in my Ministry, so I began to seek God more fervently. I called upon his name, and asked him to put his righteousness inside of me.

I have always loved television, and became what I would call a "professional television watcher." Until I began to feel I was hearing from heaven more. As a professional television watcher, I saw numerous movies. Some I liked, and some I didn't like.

When I wasn't in church services, I would sit in front of the television, and watch the old James Bond; Clint Eastwood; and John Wayne movies. I came home from work one day and prayed to God, and something amazing happened.

I felt the Holy Ghost unction telling me to pray instead of watching television, and I wanted to pray to God more. I told God, "You anointed me to preach your word so many would get saved, but I wanted more."

I began to feel I was hearing from heaven more. I prayed so much until I felt God leading me into a Consecration. He led me to go to my Pastor's study at Greater St. John FWB church and stay there all night. For 31 days I did this. At night I would lie on the floor and begin to seek the face of God. Some would say, "Why on the floor?"

It was on the floor where God taught me to pray all night. I had pain in my body from being on the floor. My body was not use to lying on the floor. As I laid there on the floor, my ribs hurt, my side hurt and my bottom hurt. I obeyed God because I wanted something from him. Therefore, I prayed to God as he had led me to do for 31 days. I had one specific prayer as I lay on the floor. I prayed to God for his healing anointing to come upon me. His word says: **"You said if there is any sick among you? Let him call for the Elders of the Church; and let them pray over him, anointing him with oil in the name of the Lord. (James 5:14).** When the "healing anointing" came upon me, I was not aware of it at the time. This is what makes the Holy Ghost so amazing.

When the Holy Ghost begins to come upon you and anoint you, you won't be aware of it. Why wouldn't you know? It's because the anointing is not yours, it belongs to God. He is the one who fills us with his power. You have got to trust through his Holy Spirit, that when he comes upon you, that you are anointed.

If we felt the anointing of God when he comes powerfully upon us, we would become self-exalted. This is the state of exalting ourselves in the presence of God. We should not do this. For 31 days I stayed in the presence of God and talked to him. My wife, Myrtle who I call Honey, brought my meals and everything else I needed to the church. After the 31 days was over, I came out and we went right in to a revival at the church. The revival lasted two weeks. While we were in revival the anointing of God was very strong when the people came around the altar. I told the people they did not have to tell me why they came to the altar. I would tell them why they came.

For two weeks they would come with problems and situations. I would lift my hands in the presence of God and the anointing would come down in my hands and all over me.

As I laid hands on the people they would be healed. A woman came from Wilmington, N.C. to the service one night. She was suffering with a back problem. While she was slain in the spirit, the power of the Holy Ghost rested on her. God healed her in a very powerful and awesome way. All the glory belongs to God for her healing.

As the healing anointing was moving through me, God was healing his people. I continued seeking God daily. In my seeking him, I could not watch television. This meant I had more time to pray and talk to God. Therefore; I prayed and talked to God. As I watched, the things I saw in the Spirit were being placed in my spirit. Now, only the word of God and his Spirit had a place inside of me.

The scriptures teach us; "It is of the Lord's mercies that we are not consumed, because his compassions fail not. They are new every morning: great is thy faithfulness." (KJV Lam. 3:22-23) We need to know there are new levels in the Spirit of God each day, but we cannot reach them doing carnal things. We must live a life of sacrifice.

God's word will teach you more concerning these things because there are higher heights and deeper depths in the Lord. He will reveal some very powerful and awesome things in your life. I could not watch television for a year, so I kept on praying, and God continued healing the people. Many people were healed, and the more he healed, the more I wanted him to heal. I felt God beginning to reveal deeper revelations concerning his people. **What's the use of having the Holy Ghost if you're not going to obey him?**

The bible tells us "Be not forgetful to entertain strangers: for thereby some have entertained angels unaware" (KJV Heb. 13:2). I remember when I was working in the barber shop and this particular man came in, amongst several other customers on this same day. The man sat in my chair. As I cut his hair, he began to minister to me about some things that would happen my life. The things he told me; I would have never dreamed of them happening to me. The entire time he sat in my chair, I was thinking, could he be an angel? There are some things about God that some people just do not believe. Pastor Mitchell believes.

This man was an elderly man with grey hair. He kept talking and in my mind I kept saying, this must be an angel. When I finished cutting his hair, he paid me, gave me a tip, and left. No one knew who this man was.

I worked at the barber shop for 17 years after this and never saw this man again. To this day I believe that he was an angel of God that came to give me a prophetic word from the Lord. God will keep preparing you repeatedly, for the things you must do for his will and his glory.

It wasn't long after the healing anointing began that I felt God dealing with me more in the Spirit. Now remember I had not been watching television for one year. When the end of that year came, the Lord dealt with me in a dream and a vision. He showed me how it was his desire for me not to return to watching television. I was sitting in the living room of our home, with my wife, watching television. The Holy Spirit came upon me and reminded me of the dream I had. At this point I felt that God did not want me to return to watching television.

I said; "God you mean that I have to go longer, and not watch television?" I could hear these words within me, "Do it for me." My eyes began to fill up with tears, and I began to say to God, "I'll do it for you." I don't know about you, but when I do something for the will of God, it really affects me and I just have to say yes. Another year passed, and I didn't watch television. Remember I was a "professional television watcher." The process kept on year after year, no television. How many years did I go and not watch television? It was ten years before I felt God had released me to watch television again.

I have learned whatever you put in your spirit man that is not of the Holy Ghost, that's what operates. You just pray and ask God to place his Holy Spirit inside of you in a very powerful way.

If you are asking him for a healing anointing, you will need the power of the Holy Ghost, because you are asking for his very essence and his presence to come and live on the inside of you. The healing anointing can only flow through a vessel that is clean and pure. God's healing anointing will flow through male or female. All that is required is that you are a pure and willing vessel. When I began seeking God, while lying on the floor; I went and purchased an air mattress, because my body hurt from lying on the floor. As I was lying on the air mattress, I felt God dealing with me, about being comfortable. Why was I trying to be comfortable? As a result, I had to get rid of the air mattress.

I reverted back to just lying on the floor and It was still very uncomfortable. I was not use to it. This was a form of God breaking me and preparing me for his will and glory, which entailed a lot of uncomfortableness.

As I traveled to other cities and states to minister God's word, I slept on the floor. I stayed in wonderful hotels, but it did not matter I had to obey God. I still laid on the floor. This was how I was instructed by God to pray all night. Many people would ask, "How do you pray all night?" My answer: "Well, on the floor after you have tossed and turn from the pains in your body all night, you automatically start praying and talking to God." Let God have his way. I think the church has missed it when it comes to praying. **Prayer is the key and Faith unlocks the door, Jesus is sitting at the right hand of the father interceding for you and I, 24 hours a day.** What makes you think we do not have to pray, and he is praying for us daily? He is a powerful and truly awesome God.

Chapter Two

Walking In God's Anointing

As I walk in this anointing that God has placed inside of me, I know that it's still increasing, because I have begun to give up a lot of things.

Honey and I, were led to go on a consecration. During this consecration I was to abstain from her for 90 days. I had to really pray. That's right, I love her very much and she is a precious jewel. I had to really fast, pray and talk to God during this consecration.

The anointing inside of me continued to increase during the consecration. Many miracles were taking place in our church services. God's hands were blessing the ministry.

As I worked in Central Heights Barber Shop and served as Pastor at Greater St. John F.W.B. Church, I still wanted more from God. If you desire more of God, he will give it to you. There are things you must do to get his anointing.

Don't seek God for houses or land and worldly possessions. **"But seek ye first the kingdom of God, and his righteousness and all things shall be added unto you." (KJV Matt. 6:33)** This is God's word and his promise, and we must be obedient to his commandments. God's anointing was increasing in my life. I was continually talking to God and his revelations were coming to me, through the Holy Spirit. By this time, I had reached the age of 33. This was a good age for me because this was the same age as Jesus, when he departed from the face of the earth.

The day I turned 33, my wife Honey and Helen Boothe, a mother of the church, took me out to dinner. We were driving home on the night of my birthday, and we were about a half mile from my home. The Holy Ghost came upon me so strongly that I fell across the steering wheel of the car. Honey called my name, "Bill, are you, all right?" I barely got the car in the driveway.

Tears were pouring from my eyes as if someone had poured a bucket of water from them. Honey asked me several times, "Are you all right." I finally said, "Yes." Help me into the house, and then to my study. Honey and Mother Boothe, both had to assist me. I was unable to walk, due to the presence of the Holy Spirit resting on me. Once I got in my study, I fell on my face and I don't know how long I was there, but the presence of God was all over me. I do not know how long I was in the Spirit, before I began to hear and feel what God was leading me to do. I felt him say: "You belong to me, and nobody can have you. Not your wife, not your mother, and not your friends. Nobody can have you. You are mine." It was then I knew I had to retire from my job, as a Master Barber. I was thinking in my mind: "Lord you are leading me to retire from my job and do full time ministry?" I had no other alternative but to retire and do God's will.

This experience happened on my birthday, February 2, 1998, at the age of 33. I shared this revelation with my wife, my mother who was also my Pastor, my father and my family at large, what I felt God was leading me to do. I told them, "I have to retire from my job and do full time ministry." Following this, I had to tell my spiritual Mother, Ms. Chanie, that I had to retire, which meant giving up the barber shop. She was the one who encouraged me to go into the Barbering profession, which is the profession from which she had retired. She responded in astonishment I told her I felt God was leading me to retire.

She said, "What!" and her next response was, "When?" I stated, "December." She asked me if I had told my church and my response was, "No." Mother Chanie said, "What are you going to do if they don't receive it?" I said, "I'm going to preach God's word even if I have to preach it in a barn!" This is how you know the Holy Ghost is leading you. I told mother Chanie she did not have to worry about the barber shop, God is going to take care of it. The power of God fell on her and she said to me; "Obey the will of God." Not only had I felt God leading me to do his will, the anointing he placed in my life dealt with others also. When will we listen, and what will it take for us to do God's will? **What's the use of having the Holy Ghost if you're not going to obey him?**

The Craziness of obeying God. When I told everyone that I was going to retire, they said I was crazy. The responses were: "Do you realize the amount of money you would be giving up?" "How will you survive?" "Some churches last and some churches fold, what are you going to do to make it?" I was listening to all the things people were saying, but I still felt God leading me to retire and do his will.

There is one thing about God and me; when I have to do his will, I try my best to be obedient to him no matter who likes it or not. It was through my obedience to him that my blessings came.

It was not hard, but times were difficult after I retired from my job. I had already made up my mind to get out of debt prior to leaving the job. It seems as soon as I said that, I felt God leading me to retire from my job. I told God yes, I will retire and that meant that my salary would be cut greatly. Although I was still trying to get out of debt, I had to obey. The tests were increasing, but I still had to obey God. My walk had to be humble in the presence of God. There's something about the Holy Ghost anointing when it leads and guides you. It causes you to walk humbly, so God can use you for his will. We need "him"; he does not need "us." But he does want to use us.

When God begin to move through you in a powerful way, do not try to rush him. Let God be God and you be the servant. Always do as the master instructs you to do. When you obey, God will start using you even more. Once you receive this power, demon forces activate themselves against you. They will come against you to try to stop or hinder you from doing God's will.

Just remember to listen to what you feel the Holy Ghost is leading you to do. He is our comforter and guide; he comes to bless us.

When you do as I did, pray and seek God for a very powerful anointing, the enemy will begin to release demonic forces to fight you. When you reach this dimension or this level in the Holy Spirit, the enemy will realize he really can't use people to discourage you. He will try to fight you in the spirit realm. Let me tell you how he will fight you. I retired as God had led me to and I was concerned about my home. My salary was reduced to half. While the enemy was trying to stop me, God was dealing with my wife. Honey had a vision. She envisioned that our refrigerator was full of food. It was running over with food. I said to Honey, "That is confirmation from God." She said, "What do you mean?"

I told her because I retired and went into ministry full time, this was God's way of letting us know that we would never run out of food, that our refrigerator will always have something in it. It may not be what we want but we will never go hungry. He was going to take care of us. As of this day, our refrigerator is still running over with food. That's a blessing from God.

If you are married the power of the Holy Ghost will lead and guide your spouse in the same direction as you. It can be vice versa. God can reveal to the wife and he can also reveal to the husband if they are both walking in the presence of God. If one spouse is saved and the other is not, then God deals with the spouse that is saved. There are exceptions to the rule. God can also place his revelation in the unsaved spouse. Never say what God cannot do. He has all power in his hands. Remember Pharaoh, eventually said leave Egypt Moses, and take all your possessions and get out. God can reveal to the unsaved and use them for his will and glory. It may be unknowingly, but it can be done.

God is now giving Honey and I, more confirmation on what we felt he was doing and saying in our lives. It has now been a year since I had retired, and I remember a man of God called me and said he had to see me. He wanted to see me before the New Year came in. When he arrived at my home, he said he was not staying long. He had a gift that he wanted to give me before the New Year. The gift was $500.00. I told God he was incredible. He gave me and Honey $500.00.

My Assistant Pastor, Doris Langston said to me; "Pastor I have money, do you need any money? I will give you some money." She gave me $500.00.

When you feel God leading you to do something, do it. Under all conditions always present God with a clean life, obey him, do his will, give him all the glory and he will bless you. The scriptures say; **"And all these blessings shall come on thee, and overtake** thee, if thou shalt hearken unto the voice of the Lord thy God" (KJV Deut. 28.2)

As I walk and obey the Lord, his presence and anointing sends more blessings my way. People would walk up to me and literally put money in my hand. They would bless my wife and I, without our saying a word. We walked by faith and not by sight. God's word says through his son Jesus; **"Let your conservations be without covetousness; and be content with such things as ye have: for he hath said, I will never leave thee, nor forsake thee."** (KJV Heb. 13:5)

"Teaching them to observe all things whatsoever I have commanded you: and lo, I am with you always, even unto the end of the world. Amen (KJV Matt. 28:20)

You can believe God's word. God is a God that cannot lie. He is so powerful in the midst of his anointing. Please pay attention to what I'm saying, I knew God would take care of us and supply our every need. Not our wants but our needs.

We both were walking in the anointing of God, my salary cut in half, I'm 33 years old and God is supplying our every need. God never ceases to amaze me.

I felt God leading and guiding me again about retirement. But it was another type of retirement. He wanted my wife to retire from her job. My thoughts were: "Wait a minute Pastor Mitchell; this is getting crazier and crazier." "You had to come off your job making plenty of money, your salary cut in half, and now he wants you to retire your wife." "How am I going to get out of debt?" It doesn't make sense I know, but God worked it out.

Through all of what we were going through we continued to pay our tithes and offerings. My salary was cut, my wife retired, and God was still bringing us out of debt. This sounds too amazing, right? We were not making a lot of money, after retirement but God began to work miracles in our life through our obedience. That's the thing about the Holy Ghost, when you obey him in his presence, he will work miracles that really don't make sense to the natural man. He takes the simple things of this world to confound the wise. When it doesn't make sense to man, it makes sense to God. He is the one who places his word in our hearts.

Chapter Three

My Consecrations

I began sensing God leading me to add something else to my Consecration. I couldn't eat in restaurants. The enemy had begun to attack my vocal cords. On one occasion, I was at a restaurant eating and almost swallowed a piece of glass that was in my food.

On another occasion, I was drinking a soda and a bumble bee fell in it and was swimming around waiting for me to take the next swallow.

As I was listening very carefully, this is what I felt God was leading me to do. I had to stop eating in restaurants and prepare my own food. I would continue to purchase my food from the grocery store. When I traveled, I still had to prepare my own food? If I had to go to restaurants, I would just sit and fellowship and watch others eat. Some would say they could not enjoy their food, and it did not taste good because the anointing they felt was so powerful coming from my life.

When I had to prepare my own food, I was being obedient to God. For three years I did not eat in restaurants. Remember I told you, when you start obeying God in the fullness of his anointing, demonic forces will start to stir up and move.

In the beginning there was no television, and now I couldn't eat in any restaurants. I considered myself to be a "professional eater" also. Yes, I loved to eat, and I think eating is so wonderful. I saw all of this as a means of God bringing more discipline in my life. The Holy Ghost is intelligent.

When you feel him leading you, just listen to him. During the time I couldn't eat out, do you know how much money we saved? We live in a day and time now, so many of us eat out almost every day. The money we saved from eating out we used it to take care of things that were needed in the home. We serve a wise and intelligent God.

Three years passed while we were trying to get out of debt, God began to do it. We had a plan and a goal in the presence of the Holy Ghost. It makes sense that when you are in Ministry full time, to only have your focus on it and not your finances. God can free up your money for paying bills and other things, so you can use it for the ministry.

When you put your money in the ministry you have to know how to sow. The bible says; **"Be not deceived; God is not mocked: for whatsoever a man soweth, that shall he also reap. (KJV Gal. 6:7)** We began to sow. You mean to tell me Pastor William A. Mitchell Jr., you retired from your job, your wife retired, with your salary cut in half, trying to get out of debt and you are still going to sow? You can't watch television, or eat in restaurants, what did you do? I learned how to touch God that he may touch me back. There are some intimate ways to touch God.

My next level of Consecration was in the old church which only seated 150 people. I was seeking God's presence which is what I love to do. I went into consecration for 61 days. I stayed in the church, without coming out the entire time. I could feel

God's love leading me to seek him. If I love him, I will seek him because he is Holy. Seemingly, I had to get in a sack cloth and ashes position or a threshing floor position to get in his presence. I remained in the church in my study which was very small, for 61 days; I could barely turn around in it. I slept on the floor and sought God. I could not be in anyone's presence, while I was in this consecration.

My wife Honey, and Mother Boothe would bring me food. They would place the food in the dining hall in the church. They would lock the door and leave. I would watch them ride off. Once they left I would leave the study to eat.

This Consecration continued through Thanksgiving, my wife's birthday, Christmas and New Year's. During this period of time I remained in the church away from my family. I felt humiliated, and very low. You will understand when I explain. There was no shower. I had to bathe from a bucket of water. All the amenities of home were lacking. Whenever I discuss these 61 days of consecration, my eyes fill with tears as a result of what I went through.

Someone called my Assistant Pastor, Doris one day and told her I was in trouble in the church and was hurting. She and her husband rushed to the church to help me. They asked if I was alright. I said yes, I'm fine, and nothing is wrong. The devil was mad because I was at the church, obeying God. Whatever God leads you to do, do it. The devil will tell you, you can't do it. If you feel led by the Holy Ghost to do a consecration don't let anything or anybody stop, you. Don't let anyone bring you out until it's time. I remember having a pain in my neck one night. The pain came from being stationary in one position and praying for a long time.

It felt like a pulled muscle. I wanted to call someone to take me to the hospital. I was in such pain that I cried. However; I made up my mind that I would not let any infirmity bring me out of the 61-day consecration. The entire time, I could see Jesus carrying the cross. I could see the blood running from his body. He was keeping us in his vision while he was on the cross. While I was in this consecration, I was keeping him in my vision. During my consecration, my associate ministers facilitated the services, I remained in my study. I could hear the services going on and the people praising God. Oh, how I wanted to be in the service, but I was being led by God to do this for him.

I remember two of my members at that time, who were very sweet, Ennis and Crystal Faison. They thought about me over the holidays and brought me barbeque and coleslaw. It touched my heart. Brother Ennis said to me, "Pastor Mitchell I could not enjoy my Christmas dinner without sharing it with you." I thanked them both for the love he and his wife Crystal had shown me.

While in the Consecration, I prayed for two or three days straight. God had taken sleep from me. I prayed and prayed, and I said, "God I have been praying to you for two or three days now. Can I go to sleep?" I had very little sleep. If I nodded off for a little while, I would wake up again and continue praying.

As I was praying on one occasion, "I said Lord I have not felt you saying anything." I kept on talking to God and he still didn't say anything. I was sitting at my desk, in that little study of mine and I said God I have been talking to you for days now and I have not felt you saying anything. I said to him, "What is it?" I was getting frustrated and angry. I said, "That's alright", and I took my hand and slammed it on the desk. "If you won't let me feel you speaking, I will just keep on praying." When those words came off my lips the power of God filled the room with a great anointing. Tears fell from my eyes. I sensed the power of the Holy Ghost all over me and it filled my study. I said, "That's it." I felt within myself, that God didn't want to say anything. He just wanted me to keep on praying. God gave me this revelation, a lot of saints stop praying, because they do not feel God moving. When you pray to God, don't look for him to move or to feel anything, right away. He's God. Just continue to pray and talk to him. When he gets ready and decides to move, you will feel him leading and guiding you.

Now when I go into intercessory prayer, I don't look for God to move right away. I just pray no matter how long it takes. When he decides to speak, he speaks and when he decides to move, he moves. He's God.

Another experience I had while I was on the 61-day Consecration in the old church. What's the use of having the Holy Ghost if you don't listen to him and obey him? On this particular day, it was cold outside, and there may have been some snow on the ground. I kept my study warm with a small electric heater. I was lying on the floor wrapped in quilts. Believe me, It was extremely cold. I prayed all day long. I said, "God from morning until now and it's night, I have not felt you saying anything." "What's going on today, with us?"

I notice while I was making these statements my lips were not moving. I had been talking in tongues all day. When I pray for a long period of time my mind begins to talk to God. Remember, God knows our thoughts before we even begin to think them. In my mind I began to talk to God. I said; "God I have been praying to you, and I have not felt you say anything." I was lying on the floor praying, and I felt his voice in my spirit saying, "You keep on touching me." I said, "What?"

I heard it again. "You keep on touching me." I said to God, "You mean the more I pray, I'm touching you?" I wept like a baby. It is our prayers, which move God.

God revealed some powerful things during this 61-day Consecration, mainly how to build the church. He even showed me my enemies, who were trying to stop us from building the new church. My enemies motivated by the devil did not want me to be successful at ministry. We shouldn't worry about those things. **"Ye are of God, little children, and have overcome them: because greater is he that is in you, than he that is in the world" (KJV 1 John 4:4)** We are more than conquerors in Christ Jesus. People talk about power and having power. Let me tell you about the Holy Ghost power. With the Holy Ghost power, you can learn how to love those who do not want to see you blessed or successful.

In a vision from God, he showed me, "Whatever you do, don't fight. I told God, "I will not fight." God will take care of everything, if you would just let him. God revealed if you let him be God, his fire can burn up everything that's not right. He can destroy everything that gets in your way.

God was still dealing with me during this 61-day consecration. He showed me all he was going to do, and how he was going to do it. I gave God thanks and praise for what he was going to do. We did not have any land to build the church. Different ones came to me to talk to me about where to build the church. I refused to talk to all of them, until God released me. I was still on my 61 day Consecration in the church. We eventually purchased the land that people said we wouldn't get to build the church. We purchased 9.8 acres. We purchased it and paid for it. While I was on my consecration, shut up in the church, God was doing some powerful things. That's the thing about the Holy Ghost, once you allow him to be in control of your life, he prepares everything for you. A lot of people do not believe this; **"But seek ye first the kingdom of God, and his righteousness; and all these things shall be added unto you." (KJV Matt. 6:33)** God is powerful and awesome. How many times have you heard this in this book?

He has been powerful in every Consecration I have been in. God leads me in every one of them. **What's the use of having the Holy Ghost if you don't obey him?**

Chapter Four

God Changed My Dialect

There was a time that we had a very powerful Holy Communion service. My mother, who I previously mentioned before was my Pastor. Her name was Hilda Mitchell, a prophet of the Lord, (who has gone home to be with the Lord). She told me in that service, "God is going to bless you."

I remember her laying hands on me, and I went in to unknown tongues. I remained in tongues most of the service. This happens to me often. When I was able to speak English again, God's anointing changed my dialect. I felt God within my spirit saying, I'm going to prove to everyone that my hands and my powerful anointing is upon you. Can you imagine a North Carolinian having a dialect like a Jamaican? When God's anointing decides to change your dialect; he does. It goes from one level to another level. What blesses me about the dialect is when I talk to people from other countries, they say I sound like them, and they like it. There are those who think my dialect is fake.

There is no way you can fake it. My dialect changed in 1999, I still have it today. When people say I'm faking it, I say well I'm a pro because I have been talking this way for about 19 years. I laugh.

God told Abraham and Sarah that they were going to have a child and they were past child bearing age. They laughed. Why does God do these things?

The Bible says; "Then said Jesus unto him, Except ye see signs and wonders, ye will not believe." (KJV John 4:48) Therefore, every time I open my mouth with this dialect, I would have to tell this amazing story. I was born and raised in North Carolina, in the good old USA. But God's anointing gave me this dialect. The people are blessed and blown away. As God increased his healing anointing in me, my dialect increased. I'm just a peculiar fellow that got a powerful anointing at a young age. Selah.

Before my Mother laid hands on me and my dialect changed, things had already begun to happen concerning my dialect. I was at the old church. Remember it only seated 150 people. I would pray with the members in intercessory prayer. God ordained this prayer at the church. We would come to the church on Saturday morning and pray for one hour.

We still have intercessory prayer to this day at the church. I was sitting in prayer and I began to tell the people to not say anything about people who speak in tongues. It's a gift. You can have it, if you desire it.

All a person has to do is continue to pray consistently and the anointing of the Baptism of the Holy Ghost will come upon you. During this particular intercessory prayer session, I was sitting in the Deacon's section of the church praying to God. As I was praying, under the anointing, I would pray in English, and then I would pray in tongues. After I prayed in this manner for an hour or more, the power of God would come on me very strongly. At that time my membership at the church was small in number.

The members would sit and listen to God pray through me by

the Holy Ghost. When the Holy Ghost was praying through me, it sounded like I was going through different countries. It sounded like I was praying in Spanish, or French. You name it. I heard many of the different dialects that you would hear internationally. The prayer would come out of me as the sound of living waters. The scripture says, **"He that believeth on me, as the scripture hath said, out of his belly shall flow rivers of living waters." (KJV John 7:38)** That's more than one river.

As I was praying, out of my belly flowed rivers of living waters. God can change your dialect, and he can give you multiple gifts in the Holy Spirit. While I was praying, the sounds of the different nationalities would come out of me. My members thought that it was strange and somewhat peculiar, but they knew their Pastor was submitted under God's power. I noticed that when the anointing would come upon me strongly, I would have a very proper accent, when I preach, teach, or talk. God was preparing the Church for what he was going to do in their Pastor. After God changed my dialect, the members could reflect back on what God had shown them.

God will reveal some things to you, to bless your life in your present, and take you into your future. You will read this again in this book, **God will explain your past, teach you your present and reveal to you your future. The only way he can explain your past, is after you have gone through some things with the Holy Ghost. Then he will begin to teach you in your present about your past. While he is teaching you about your present, he will reveal to you your future.**

He reveals your future in your past, and you don't understand it, until you get to your present. **"Jesus Christ the same yesterday,**

and to day, and for ever. (KJV Heb. 13:8) This is what the scripture says.

My dialect began to change vigorously. I felt God in my spirit saying "I'm going to prove to the world that my anointing is upon you. I'm going to show them that you are my chosen one. "There are many chosen by God.

On another occasion when the Spirit was moving in the service, I felt the Lord saying, "Before you leave this world, people will know that you were chosen by the almighty God." God speaks to me through his Spirit in a very potent way. For this I give him praise, honor and glory.

The anointing on me, continued to increase, and as it increased so did the members of the church, that only seated 150 people. I remember leaving out of a business meeting one night before it was over because, the Holy Ghost fell on me. As I walked towards my Pastor's study, God led me to tell the people, "Other people are coming." "Move over, slide over, prepare for them." "They are coming." Then I walked into my study. In a very short time, people began to come from everywhere. They kept coming. I began to preach more powerfully than ever. I love God, and I love God's people. I told God I wanted to do many great things for him.

During this walk with God as I preached, the anointing got intense, and I received much revelation. The people were coming from near and far. A statement was made about our Sunday morning services by other people in the neighborhood. They said, "Pastor Mitchell needs to please make some arrangements to get all the members in the parking lot." In a humorous way another lady said, "On my way to Church I can't get past Greater St. John F.W.B. Church for so many cars turning in the parking lot." The people kept coming. The seating capacity at the old church was

150 to 175. During our church services people would stand around the walls, in the foyer and wherever they could. You would find children seated on the altar. What are you saying Pastor Mitchell? I am saying the Holy Ghost was so powerful that we had to go to two services on Sunday?

We had an 8 a.m. service and an 11 a.m. service to accommodate the people. The anointing was equally powerful in both services. The sermons preached were tailored differently for each service. Very seldom have I preached the same Sermon after preaching for 37 years. My Sermons have always been different. When I preached the anointing continued to increase. In the services people were getting healed, delivered and set free.

Chapter Five

God's Powerful Healing Anointing

I remember a Holy Communion service at my home church, Revelation Mission. The current Pastor is Dr. Juanita Whitfield, my dear sweet sister.

After the service, before I left the church; the Holy Ghost fell on me very strongly and this is what I felt God was leading me to say, "Somebody is going to be healed on tomorrow in your service at Greater St. John. Somebody is going to be healed tomorrow in the service." I spoke these very words at Revelation Mission, "God is going to heal somebody in the service on tomorrow at Greater St. John."

I did not know who it was going to be. The next day the church service was powerful. We were going deeper in the presence of the Holy Ghost.

Prepare yourself for this spiritual journey as God enlighten you about the Holy Spirit and how he can bless you. You have got to believe what he says and know that it's not given to you to always understand. Just trust what the Holy Ghost leads and guide you to do.

We were in that particular service that the Lord had alluded to the night before. That morning the power of God was ever present. A mother of one of the members fell over in the pew. I was told, by members in the church that there was someone visiting that worked in the medical field, that stated: "She is gone." "She has no pulse." 911 was called. I stood there and told the congregation to relax and stay calm. I didn't even lay hands on her to pray for her. As I stood there, the Holy Ghost brought back to my remembrance, what was placed in my spirit the night before at the Holy Communion service, at Revelation Mission. "Pastor on tomorrow at Greater St. John somebody is going to be healed." The paramedics arrived, and they proceeded doing CPR on her. I continued to stand there. I was not emotional. I was calm. I said, "God what are you going to do?"

Here we are. The mother is lying there on the pew. She is turning cold. She is gone. No pulse. "Now God, what are you going to do?" "Is she going to be healed? I'm waiting on you". I was saying all this to myself. About that time, you could hear her take a deep breath and she began to come back to us. The woman that was visiting the church who told me the mother had had no pulse, that she was gone, stood up and said; "I'm telling you all, this woman was gone." "She had no pulse." "Nothing." "God brought her back." Well, what do you think we did after that? The church began to give God praise, honor and glory and thanked him for what he had done.

This was not the first time God raised somebody that died or had no pulse in my presence. I remember being in a service at our United American Free Will Baptist Tabernacle headquartered in Kinston NC, under the leadership of Bishop J.E. Reddick. One of my members was sitting on the back pew of the tabernacle and fell over. They said he was gone, and he had no pulse. His wife rushed to get me.

I went to him and laid my hands on his chest and began to pray for him. Suddenly, his eyes open and he said, "I don't know what happened, but when I woke up my Pastor's hands was on my chest and I was breathing." How does this story end? This member lived a long time after this incident.

When God moves in a powerful way and uses us, why can't we just believe in him and trust what he does? God is waiting for us to step up in the realm of the Spirit with him, so that he may lead and guide us into plain truths and plain paths.

Pastor Mitchell is a man that believes God no matter what he says. I believe him and trust him with every fiber of my being. I don't have to ask anyone will God do it, I just know because I've seen him do it. He has done so many things in the midst of his anointing, and I give him all the praise, glory and honor.

There was a young person who was coming to the church that had been afflicted with AIDS. I prayed for their healing. When they returned to the doctor, the doctor told them there were no signs of the disease. They tested them and could find no evidence of the disease in their body. The doctor told the person this was the first time he had seen this. The young person got saved and joined the church.

They eventually left the church and went back out in the world and resumed their previous life style. They no longer lived for the Lord. After a year or so later, they were again diagnosed with AIDS and was told it was spreading. For the life of me, I cannot figure out, why do we come and get one miracle from God and don't keep coming back for more miracles? Why settle for just one when you can have so much more. It's as if, we want God to bless us only in this dilemma, and we go back to what we were doing until we need him for the next tragedy in our life. Then we want God to come again and bless us. How is it, that we can't live for God and do what he wants us to do, and receive all his blessings and miracles. I'm so glad he is a merciful yet powerful God.

We were having revival at the old church and the power of the Holy Ghost came upon me. A visitor in the service was sitting in the back of the church. She had been in abusive situations and she had disabilities in her body. I began to speak the word of God to her through the Holy Ghost. She came in with a cane and I told her that God was going to heal her that night. She had experienced much trauma in her life, along with the physical disabilities. She stayed at home a lot because she had problems moving about. She had a loving husband that took care of her.

As she began to listen to me it was as if someone hit her head with a baseball bat. She fell over in the pew as I gave her that prophetic word, that God was leading me to tell her. When she got up, she came to me and told me God had healed her. She expressed to me all that God's power had done for her. After the service she left the church. I did not see her for a while.

I said to myself, if I was in a place and I had infirmities in my body, and had received a miracle that healed me I would still be there. I would wait to see what God would do next.

This is what I'm trying to tell you: When the Holy Ghost blesses your life in a very mighty way, why not seek him more to find out where you need to be, to get the rest of your miracles. When you have tough problems and issues going on in your life, the Holy Ghost can deliver you out of them all. **We need to be like Apostle Paul; "I press toward the mark for the prize of the high calling, of God in Christ Jesus. (KJV Phil. 3:14)** I later found out, that this lady had been trying to find her way back to the church. She came as a visitor that night. She was not a member. The word is true, all things do work together for the good of them that love the Lord and are called according to his purpose. She made it back to the church and joined our church. She remained at the church until she relocated to another state.

At another time in revival, a woman attended from Wilmington, North Carolina. She drove about one hour and thirty-minutes to our church. She was experiencing back problems and she wanted to be healed. I laid hands on her and she went out under the power of God. God healed her back. Her blessings didn't just stop there. Her blessings began to come, and they kept on coming.

In Washington, North Carolina, I was preaching under a powerful anointing and the devil tried to do everything he could to stop me. The enemy was attacking my life. This was a very devastating time in my life. I did not want to preach God's word anymore. I did not want to be around church people anymore.

I remember saying I do not want to do this. You know as well as I do the devil can do some things that are hurtful and painful, and I was going through the trial of my Faith.

I'm standing in a church in Washington, N.C., and the only reason I was there was because of a promise I made. I promised God that I would preach his word until I die. The enemy was trying to destroy me through the traumas I was having in my own personal life.

You are probably thinking in your minds, "Well, Pastor Mitchell what did you do?" To give you a better revelation, I was like the servant Job. I was trying to live the best I knew how, but the enemy was trying to destroy me. My spirit was saying, go ahead Devil, take your best shot, I will survive. My flesh was in total contrast. Here I am, at this church and not wanting to be there. As I said before, I was there because of an appointment and a promise. I was not feeling anything. I was torn and heart ripped, but I had promised God. As I began to minister the word, this service turned out to be one of the most powerful services I had ever experienced.

I began to prophesy to a woman in the service. I told her, "I see you getting out of that wheelchair."

She had two strokes that had affected one side of her body, but she was still praising God. The more God blessed the service, the more I felt like I did not want to be there. I told God, "I do not want to do this, but I made you a promise." That's what I kept saying to God. "I made you a promise." Before I knew it, in the multitude of people the woman stood up in the back of the church, kicked the wheelchair out from under her, and she was praising God. I jumped up stood on the Bishop chair and looked down the aisle and she was shouting.

I said to the congregation, "Look! The woman is out of her wheelchair shouting and praising God." This woman is still doing well, from the last report I received. Did this make me feel better? Just a little. Pain hurts when it is deep rooted, and you didn't ask for it.

I started to walk on the promise that I made to God. **"Let your conservation be without covetousness and be content with such things as ye have: for he hath said, I will never leave thee, nor forsake thee." (KJV Heb. 13:5)**

God will be with you to the end of the world. I did not want to preach and tell the goodness of the Lord, because of the attack of the enemy on my life.

This will happen to all us, in some way or fashion. It was hard, but God made it powerful. I was determined to stay saved and live for God.

Well, Pastor Mitchell how could you experience all of that and still not want to be in the service? When you are hurting and in pain, you don't care. But there is something about the power of the Holy Ghost.

Not only will he lead and guide you, but he will comfort you. The scripture tells us he is a Comforter. The more work I did for God, the more he healed me. I stayed in church and he blessed me.

I never stopped loving his people and I never stopped doing what he had called me to do. I consider myself to be a man of integrity. I didn't know when he would do it, but I knew he would do it. I loved God so much and I knew he would do it for me just like he did it for his servant Job. I was just waiting on the manifestation of my healing.

At Greater St. John F.W.B. Church, I felt God leading me to tell the church he wanted us to bring in 100 souls in 31 days.

We had to go out and bring 100 souls to the kingdom of God. I explained to the membership, we will do this for God, 100 souls in 31 days. I told the church; our community is different from larger cities. We are located near the small town of Dudley, N.C. Therefore, we will have to go out to other areas. I would leave church during the week, and go out, then come back to the church on Sunday morning to preach the word.

I told the church to listen to me, because we have specific instructions. Only go into the homes of people that invite you. Don't force yourself on anyone, and in their home. Don't attempt to tell them a lot of things. My goal as Pastor would be to pray with them; tell them about the goodness of the Lord; and to believe God for their miracles. I was going after Souls. We were not going in their homes unless they are willing to invite us. This is what's wrong with the church today. We try to force Jesus on the people. Jesus never forced himself on anyone. He presents himself through the power of God. He came so powerfully the people could not resist him. At this point, I began to train my members how to go out and witness and minister to the people in their homes.

We evangelized all over. We even ventured down to Washington, N.C. and stayed all day ministering to people. The power of God moved. Miracles on top of Miracles happened. People were saved, healed, and delivered.

Pastor Mitchell and the church did as God had led them to do. The vision was to bring in 100 souls to God's kingdom in 31 days. We did just what was asked, within 31 days. On the last Saturday which was the 31st day, we held a street ministry in front of one of my young members' home. This member lived in the inner part of the city.

On that Saturday many souls came to the Lord. **107 Souls were saved during those 31 days.** God is amazing.

I must ask this question; "When the Holy Ghost comes to us in a powerful way, why do we turn our face from him?" God is so loving and kind that he sent his only son that whosoever believes in him will be saved.

I remember we went to a young woman's home when we were out ministering for the 31 days. She was in a wheelchair. I began to minister to her while she was sitting in her wheelchair.

While I was ministering to her, she was also thinking about her living situation.

She was living with her boyfriend. In her conservation she began to say she did not want to get saved right now. I said, "Can I just pray for you?" Her reply was, "Yes." I prayed for her and after the prayer her legs came out of the wheelchair. That's right they just popped out. She stood up for the first time. I said, "Would you look at this miracle." I asked her, "After this miracle that God gave you, don't you want to serve him so you can receive more miracles?" You know what she told me, "No, I'm going to wait for my boyfriend to get saved." I told her it's alright the choice is yours. I did not force her. God is just that kind of God.

When you turn your back on God, or say you don't want his anointing and blessings, you better be prepared for what might come later.

The scriptures say, **"For he is our God; and we are the people of his pasture, and the sheep of his hand. To day if ye will hear his voice, harden not your heart, as in the provocation, and as in the day of temptation in the wilderness". (KJV Psalm 95:7-8)** What happened to this woman? It was only a few weeks later that I received a report that the woman had died. This young woman did not want to get saved after God had given her a miracle right in her home, because she did not want to give up her boyfriend.

"If thou shalt confess with thy mouth the Lord Jesus and shalt believe in thine heart that God has raised him from the dead, thou shalt be saved". (KJV Rom 10:9)

Jesus died on the cross and was raised from the dead and sits at the right hand of the father, with that confession you must believe in your heart, then you shall be saved. If she didn't confess this with her mouth before she died, she is in hell today, because she was trying to hang on to a boyfriend. **Selah (think on these things)**

I have a lot of spiritual children and one of my spiritual daughters was on her way home from school one day. She notices a lady and a man standing in a yard.

They waved at her, so she waves back. They did not know each other. Somehow this spiritual daughter ended up at their house. She was just passing by. There was no stop light or stop sign. I believe she felt led by God to stop. This occurred during the time of our 31 days of winning souls. Their mother was in the home and she suffered from a stroke.

When my spiritual daughter went in the home, she saw the woman in a wheelchair. Her son and daughter were also in the home. The daughter had move from a Northern state to take care of her mother.

My spiritual daughter told them her Pastor was visiting people's homes and praying for them. She said: "You need to ask him to come and pray for your mother." They contacted me and I went to their home to pray. The daughter had gone to the store, but the son was at home. We prayed, and the power of God came upon the mother so strongly, she got up and walked around. Her son looked on with amazement. When the daughter got home her brother told her all about what God had done. She said, "so mom got up and walked." She didn't believe. She said, "Something is wrong with all of you." At that time her mom popped up and walked. She was tired but she gave God the praise. The end of this story is the daughter who move home to North Carolina to take care of her mom, went back to her home. Her Mother was able to take care of herself.

Final Note to the Leaders

God is a miracle working God and he is very awesome and powerful. The things that I, Pastor Mitchell have talked about in this book are experiences that the Lord gave me through the power of the Holy Ghost. These are just a few.

God is always preparing us to minister in the church and be a blessing to the people. It was God through his son and the Holy Spirit, who was teaching me how to move in the anointing that he has placed within my life. I have shared different things that happened concerning God's healing power.

What we must learn is how God will speak through us, how he will move through us and how he will lead and guide us. Sometimes it comes through trial and error. Sometimes it comes through praying and talking to God. Once you get it, you got it and that's good. Many things happen in the anointing of God, people get healed, delivered and set free.

God does not move through me the same way all the time. He will not move through you the same way all the time. Learn how to be versatile, and how to use the gifts he has placed on the inside of you.

The word of God teaches us that out of our belly shall flow rivers of living waters. Pray that God will speak and move through you that all his people will be blessed. All the things that I have placed in this book are tools to prepare you to minister to the needs others. I pray you learn how healings and blessings come. I hope you can see how the Holy Spirit taught me regarding different personalities in the lives of the people. We must attain knowledge from God to know how to minister to others. You can do this through the Holy Ghost. Remember the Holy Ghost can teach you all things.

Learn how to flow and change what the enemy has planned for your life and others. When you learn to do this, you are close to mastering the use of the gift that God has placed inside of you, the Holy Ghost. When I say master the use of the gift this means learn of him. Nobody is the true master, except God the Father, God the Son and God the Holy Ghost.

What's the use of having the Holy Ghost if you're not going to obey him?

Printed in the United States
By Bookmasters